Address to the Inhabitants of the Colonies Established in New South Wales And Norfolk Island

Richard Johnson

Alpha Editions

This Edition Published in 2021

ISBN: 9789354595448

Design and Setting By
Alpha Editions
www.alphaedis.com
Email – info@alphaedis.com

TO ALL INHABITANTS,
AND ESPECIALLY TO THE
UNHAPPY PRISONERS AND CONVICTS
ESTABLISHED AT PORT JACKSON
AND
NORFOLK ISLAND,
THIS AFFECTIONATE ADDRESS
IS DEDICATED AND PRESENTED,
BY THEIR VERY SINCERE
AND SYMPATHIZING FRIEND,
AND FAITHFUL SERVANT,
IN THE GOSPEL OF CHRIST,
RICHARD JOHNSON.

TO THE BRITISH AND OTHER EUROPEAN INHABITANTS OF NEW SOUTH WALES AND NORFOLK ISLAND

My Beloved,

I do not think it necessary to make an apology for putting this Address into your hands; or to enter into a long detail of the reasons which induced me to write it.

One reason may suffice. I find I cannot express my regard for you, so often, or so fully, as I wish, in any other way.

On our first arrival in this distant part of the world, and for some time afterwards, our numbers were comparatively small; and while they resided nearly upon one spot, I could not only preach to them on the Lord's day, but also converse with them, and admonish them, more privately.

But since that period, we have gradually increased in number every year (notwithstanding the great mortality we have sometimes known) by the multitudes that have been sent hither after us. The colony already begins to spread, and will probably spread more and more every year, both by new settlements formed in different places under the crown, and by a number of individuals continually becoming settlers. Thus the extent of what I call my parish, and consequently of my parochial duty, is enlarging daily. On the other hand, my health is not so good, nor my constitution so strong, as formerly. And therefore I feel it impracticable, and impossible for me, either to preach, or to converse with you so freely, as my inclination and affection would prompt me to do.

I have therefore thought it might be proper for me, and I hope it may prove useful to you, to write such an Address as I now present you with. I transmitted a copy of it to my friends in England with a request, that if they approved of it, a sufficient number might be printed, and sent to me. Thus I am now able to leave with you a testimony of my affection for you, and of my sincere and heart-felt concern, for your BEST, because your ETERNAL, welfare. My times are in the hand of God. He, and He only, knows how long I may live, or how long my present connection with you, may continue. I trust, however, that so long as the all-wise Disposer of all events shall be pleased to spare my life, and strength; and government shall deem my services in this remote land, necessary, it will still be, as it has hitherto been, my most ardent desire, my uniform endeavour, and my greatest pleasure, to promote your happiness. And when recalled to my native country, or removed by my God to my eternal home, to receive that crown of righteousness, which I humbly trust is laid upon me, by reading and carefully perusing the following pages, I hope you will be convinced, and reminded how sincerely you were pitied, and how dearly beloved by

Richard Johnson.
Port Jackson, Oct. 30. 1792.

At this date, exclusive of those who died or were born on the voyage from England:

Baptisms.....226

Marriages....220

Burials......854

ADVERTISEMENT

The author hopes that all well-disposed persons will excuse the imperfections they may meet in this Address. It is the first time of his appearance in print, and may be the last. Nor would he have attempted it now, were it not for the very peculiar situation he is in, and the hope he entertains, that his feeble, but he trusts, sincere, attempt, may, by the blessing of God, be made useful to those unhappy persons, with whom he is so nearly connected, and for whose salvation and happiness he is so deeply concerned.

And he returns his most sincere and hearty thanks to true Christians of every denomination, for their kind remembrance of him at the throne of grace. He still hopes, because he still needs, a continuance of their fervent prayers to God for him, that he may be indued with those gifts, and with that wisdom, zeal, and faithfulness which are so needful to direct, support, and strengthen him—and may be favoured with more manifold and abundant success in that arduous, trying, yet honourable, and at times he can say, pleasant and delightful work, in which he is engaged.

ADDRESS, &c.

PART I

I Beseech you, brethren, suffer this word of exhortation. Your souls are precious. They are precious in the sight of God. They are precious to the Lord Jesus Christ. They are precious in my esteem. Oh that you yourselves were equally sensible of their value.

We have now been here almost five years. During this time, I trust, I have been faithful in the discharge of my duty, faithful to my God, my country, my conscience, and to your immortal souls.

I would, nay I do, humbly hope, that my labours have not been wholly in vain. Some of you, I trust, have been convinced of your folly, sin and danger; you have earnestly sought, and happily found mercy with God through a Mediator. You can now approach him as a God reconciled, a merciful Father and Friend, and are evidencing the reality of you conversion, by an upright life and conversation.

But I must express my fear, that those of you, who are thus convinced of sin, and converted to God, and reformed from your evil courses, are comparatively very few. It is too evident, that the far greater part of you discover no concern for religion. The Great God, the Lord Jesus Christ, the Holy Spirit, death, judgment, eternity, heaven and hell,—these are subjects which seldom, if at all, engage your attention; and therefore you spend days, weeks, months and years, in a profane and careless manner, though you are repeatedly informed and reminded in the most plain, faithful, and alarming language I can use, that the wages of sin, without repentance, is death,[Rom. vi. 23.] the curse of God, and the eternal ruin and damnation of your souls!

Oh, I intreat you, brethren, to consider what is contained in these two words, SALVATION and DAMNATION! The one implies every thing that an immortal soul can want or desire to make it happy. The other includes an idea, the most gloomy and dreadful that can be conceived. The former will be the admiration of angels, and the song and joy of the redeemed; the latter will be the torment of devils, and of all impenitent sinners, for ever and ever [1 Pet. i. 12.; Rev. vii. 9-17.; Rev. xiv. 11.].

Remember likewise, that ere long, either this endless inconceivable happiness, or unutterable misery will be your portion, or your doom, and mine. Our glass of life is running away apace. Our time is fast hastening to a period. Death is making sure and speedy strides towards us daily, judgment is at hand, and the judge himself is at the door. And oh! consider, when the breath we now draw shall depart, the tender thread of life be cut, our state will be unalterably and for ever fixed; either to live with God, with angels, and glorified saints, in heaven; or to dwell with devils, in the darkness and torments of hell.

On these accounts your souls are, as I have already observed, very precious, not only in the sight of God, but also to me. My brethren, God is my record, how greatly I long after you all, in the bowels of Jesus Christ.[Phil. i. 8.] Next to the salvation of own foul, nothing in this world lies so near my heart, as the conversion and salvation of my fellow creatures; and especially of you, over whom I am appointed more immediately to watch, as one who must give an account [Heb. xiii. 17.].

And oh, my friends, if this affectionate, though plain address, should answer my ardent wishes and prayers, if it should prove the happy means of converting even one soul to God, I should indeed rejoice, as one that findeth great spoil [Ps. cxix. 162.]. For once, at least, endeavour to lift up your hearts with me in prayer to Almighty God, the bountiful giver of all grace. He only can make this or any other means effectual; and should it please Him of his abounding mercy to make a saving impression upon your hearts, you will reap the happy fruits of it in life, at death, and to eternity. Oh that the gracious spirit of the Lord may open the eyes and the ears of all who may read or hear what I am writing. May they who are asleep, awake! May they who are spiritually dead, be made alive!

May backsliders from God be reclaimed! May every one be stirred up to consider, What will become of him in another world! For who amongst us can dwell with everlasting burnings? [Isa. xxxiii. 14.] Yet such MUST be our lot, unless we repent. May the Lord God give, to each of you, repentance unto life, that you may be holy in this world, and happy in that which is to come!

My brethren, I trust I can say in truth, and with a sincere conscience, That I am not ashamed of the gospel of Christ.[Rom. i. 16.] It is a knowledge, and I hope an inward experience of this precious gospel, that bears up my spirits when I am ready to sink as in deep waters, and when I am almost overwhelmed by the many heavy and daily trials, crosses, difficulties and disappointments, that I meet with in this, alas! most uncomfortable situation. An acquaintance with this gospel, an experience of its truth and power, sweetens every bitter, makes my crosses comforts, and my losses gains. It is by this knowledge that I am enabled to bear the cross of Christ, not only with some degree of patience and resignation, but at some seasons, with consolation and joy; while I at one time reflect on what our dear Lord and Saviour endured for me, and at another anticipate the unspeakable honour and pleasure, which, through grace, I hope ere long to enjoy at his right hand for evermore. And to endeavour to bring you, my dear friends, to a saving knowledge of what is contained in this gospel, is not only my duty and inclination as a minister, but also my earnest desire and pleasure, and that which I long for more than for any other thing that can be named.[Rom. x. 1.]

I have often explained to you, according to my sentiments, what is contained in the gospel. But as I fear, and am indeed well aware, that many of you, after all you have heard, still remain ignorant, I will now tell you again briefly and plainly, what my views of the gospel are; that by putting this book into your hands, you may, if you please, more carefully and attentively examine and search for yourselves, whether what I lay before you be agreeable to the holy scriptures, or otherwise; and consequently, whether you ought to believe, or to reject it.

The gospel, I conceive, in its most extensive sense, comprehends the whole revealed will of God, recorded in the holy scriptures of the Old and New Testament [Tim. iii. 16.].

This sacred book, which we call the Bible, describes the original state of man, as a state of perfect purity and innocence. He was made in the image of God. He was made upright [Gen. i. 26, 27.; Eccles. vii.

29.]. His understanding, will, his affections and conscience, his body and soul, were free from defilement, guilt, or guile, and while he continued so, he was not liable to pain, misery, or death.

But man did not continue in this state. Our first parents disobeyed their Maker. By sinning against God they lost their original righteousness, and became earthly, sensual, devilish. Such are all his posterity: for who can bring a clean thing out of an unclean? Man is now the very reverse of what he was when first created. His understanding [2 Cor. iv. 5; Ephes. iv. 18.; Titus i. 15.; rom. viii.7.] is darkened, yea darkness itself; his will, his carnal mind, is enmity against God; his conscience is defiled; his affections, no longer fixed upon God his Creator and Benefactor, are engrossed by the vain and perishing things of this world; by sin his body is become mortal. Subject to pain, disease, and death [Rom. v. 12.]; and his soul is exposed to the displeasure of God, and to the curse annexed to the transgressions of his holy law. All this misery is implied in that awful threatening, In the day that thou eatest thereof thou shalt surely die[Gen. ii. 17.].

And is not this threatening, at least in part, already put into execution? Whence is there so much ignorance and contempt of God? Why do mankind so eagerly, so universally pursue the vain pleasures and follies of the world, while they seldom think of God their Maker? From whence proceed the infidelity, blasphemy, lying, theft, sabbath-breaking, slandering and the many horrid evils, which every where abound? Whence is it that so many in this colony, labour under such sore and complicated disorders, pains, and miseries? Why are so many, both young and old, taken away by death? And why is it that others who see all those things, do not take warning by them, to prepare for their own latter end? Brethren, all these are so many undeniable proofs and evidences of what I have said; namely, that we are fallen and guilty creatures. These are the effects of Adam's sin and disobedience. The certain consequences of which would have been unavoidable and endless misery, both of soul and body, to himself and all his posterity, had not some means been provided, some way laid open, for his and their recovery.

But, blessed be God, a door of hope is opened by the gospel for miserable sinners! A gracious promise was given early, even to our first parents, immediately after their fall. The seed of the woman shall break the serpent's head [Gen. iii. 15.]. This promised seed is the Lord Jesus Christ, who, in due time, was to appear in the world, to be born of a woman, that by his life, sufferings, and obedience unto death, he might recover fallen man from the misery and ruin in which he was involved. Brethren, this gospel which, as the ministers and ambassadors of God, we are commissioned and commanded to preach to sinners, proposes a free and gracious pardon to the guilty, cleansing to the polluted, healing to the sick, happiness to the miserable, light for those who sit in darkness, strength for the weak, food for the hungry, and even life for the dead [Gal. iv. 4, 5.; Gal. iii. 13.; I John i. 7.; Matt. xi. 28.; Matt. xi. 5.].

All these inestimable blessings are the fruits and effects of the death and mediation of Jesus Christ. His great design in coming into the world was to seek and to save those who are lost[Luke xviii. 10.; I Tim. i. 15.]; he came from heaven, that he might raise us to those holy and happy mansions; he endured the curse, that we might inherit the blessing; he bore the cross, that we might wear the crown; he died, that we might live; he died, the just for the unjust, that he might bring us to God [1 Pet. iii. 18.].

These blessings become ours, only by believing, or faith. Thus it is said, God so loved the world, that he gave his only begotten Son For what purpose? Why, That whosoever BELIEVETH in him should not perish, but have everlasting life [John iii. 16,18.],—he that believeth in him is not condemned; he that believeth in him who juftifieth the ungodly, his faith is counted to him for righteousness [Rom. iv. 3, 6.]. My friends, search the scriptures, and you will find that this is the tenor of the whole Bible; I may add of our church also, in the Articles and Homilies. This believing is sometimes called a coming to Christ, a looking unto Christ, a trusting in him, a casting our burden upon him [John vi. 37.; Isa. xlv. 22.; Eph. i. 12.; Ps. lv. 22.]. And remember, that until we do thus come to Christ, trust in him, cast our cares and burdens upon him, we have no part or interest in what the gospel unfolds and offers; however others, who have believed, and daily act faith upon him, are rejoicing in the participation of those rich benefits and blessings which the gospel freely offers to guilty and perishing sinners.

The faith whereby a sinner receives Christ, and becomes a partaker of all the blessings of the gospel, is the sole gift of God, wrought in the heart by his Holy Spirit [Eph. ii. 8.]. This Holy Spirit produces an inward change in the soul, called, in the scripture, the new birth, regeneration [John iii. 3-7], or conversion, and thus enables a sinner, convinced of his sin and misery, to look to Jesus, and to believe on him.

But though repentance and faith are the gifts of God, which none can obtain by any endeavours of their own, yet we are encouraged and commanded to pray for them [Luke xi. 17.].

All who have thus, through grace, believed, and are daily living a life of faith in the Son of God, shall be saved: but such as carelessly neglect, or wilfully reject this gospel must be damned [Mark xvi. 15.]. Think, I beseech you, of this! Remember, that it is the solemn declaration of the Lord Jesus Christ himself.

Now is the time to obtain the blessings revealed in the gospel, and which are set before you when it is preached. Many have had these gracious declarations made to them, before we were born, and they will be repeated to many after we are dead. But THIS is our day. NOW is the accepted time, now is the day of salvation [1 Cor vi. 2.]. TO-DAY—for you and I may not live to see to-morrow. TO-DAY; if you will hear his voice, harden not your hearts [Heb. iii. 7, 8.]. My brethren, it is your duty, your wisdom, and will finally prove to be your greatest happiness, to seek an interest in this salvation for yourselves. It is your personal, and must be your heart concern, to make your calling and election sure [2 Pet. i. 10.].

For death will soon put a period to all the overtures of grace and mercy, with which many, and particularly YOU, are now favoured. It is as I have said, both my duty and my pleasure, to preach and proclaim these glad tidings. But to whom? Not to the dead, but to the living; even to you [Acts xv. 22.]. To you is the word of the salvation sent. But, alas! should you still put it from you, and should death at last find you in an unprepared state, it will then be too late for you to begin to cry for mercy [Eccl. ix. 10.].

A day is likewise coming, when our mortal bodies, which must shortly moulder into dust, will be raised again from the dead. Whether believers or unbelievers, whether saints or sinners, we must all appear before the judgment-seat of Christ [2 Cor. v. 10.; Dan. 12.2.; Matt. xxv.21.]. For the Lord Jesus will shortly appear in the clouds of heaven, the last trumpet shall sound, the graves shall open, the sea give up her dead, and all who have lived upon earth, from the creation to the final consummation of time, will then be judged, and rewarded or punished according to their works. Mark well St. John's representation of this solemn transaction, "I saw the dead, small and great, stand before God, and the books were opened, and another book was opened, which is the book of life, and the dead were judged out of those things which were written in the books, according to their works"[Rev. xx. 12, 13.]. Such are the declarations of scripture respecting this awful season! Sinners, whatever you may now think of these things, or think or say of me, for declaring them to you, in this, plain and solemn manner, I must and will tell you, that there is not a profane oath which you have uttered, nor a lie which you have told, nor a sabbath which you have broken, nor a single act of adultery, fornication, theft, or any wickedness of which you have been guilty; in a word, there is not an evil you have committed, nor a duty you have omitted to perform, but what is noted down in the book of God's remembrance, and will be produced against you in the day of judgment, unless you repent, and believe the gospel. You must then give an account how you improved the advantages now afforded you, for attending to the things pertaining to your peace. If you do not improve them, the Bible will condemn you, every faithful sermon you have heard will condemn you, nay, every sermon which you might have heard, but would not, because you despised and neglected the ordinances of public worship, will condemn you: And alas! this address, by which I try to warn you, because I love you, and wish well to your souls; which you are now reading, or perhaps, about to throw aside with scorn, will then condemn you. The admonitions, intreaties, prayers, and tears of godly parents, the advice and reproofs of pious friends, the warning and expostulations of faithful ministers, will all witness against you. My brethren, what shall I say? The law of God, the gospel, saints, sinners, angels, your own consciences, the Holy Spirit, the Lord Jesus, the great Judge himself, will all witness against you, for your contempt and neglect of that mercy and salvation, which are set before you in the gospel.

Then all ungodly and impenitent sinners, being tried, cast, and condemned, must hear that final terrible sentence pronounced upon them, Depart, ye cursed, into everlasting fire, prepared for the devil and his angels![Matt. xxv. 41.] And remember that those who have been your associates in wickedness here, will then be your companions in misery. This will, if possible, aggravate your torment. You and they will rue the day when you first met; and mutually charge the ruin of your souls upon each other. Oh, think of this, and pray for grace to repent, before it be too late!

At that solemn season, the righteous shall be publicly and fully acquitted before the assembled world. The judge will say to them, Come, ye blessed of my Father, inherit the kingdom prepared for you, from the foundation of the world [Matt. xxv.34.]. The holy angels will then conduct them to the mansions of eternal bliss. Happy souls! They will then have no more cause to weep and mourn, to fight and wrestle. They will no more be exercised with darkness or temptation; for sin, which is the cause of all their conflicts and sorrows, shall be done away; and God their gracious Father, and everlasting Friend, shall wipe all tears from their eyes [Rev. vii. 17.].

The righteous, however obscured and reproached upon earth, shall then shine forth like the sun in the kingdom of their Father. They are represented to us, as standing before the throne, clothed in white robes, with palm-branches (the emblems of victory) in their hands, and singing to their harps their Redeemer's praise [Matt. xiii.43.; Rev vii. 9,10.]. There they will join in company with Abraham, Isaac, and Jacob, with the apostles, prophets, and martyrs, with their dear friends and relatives, who died in the faith before them, and with the glorious angels; and above all, (without which heaven itself would be no heaven to them) they will enjoy the unclouded presence of their Lord and Saviour, who once suffered pain, and shame, and death for them. They will see him seated upon a throne of glory, and unite with all the heavenly host, in ascribing salvation, glory, and honour, and praise to him who loved them, and washed them from their sins in his own blood; and has made them kings and priests to God, and to the Lamb, for ever and ever [Rev. v. 9.].

For the joys of heaven, and the pains of hell will be eternal. Otherwise, indeed, neither the happiness nor the misery of a future state could be complete. It would damp the joys of the blessed, to apprehend that they must at length terminate. And the horrors of the damned would be in a degree alleviated, if there was the most distant prospect that they would have a period. But the word of God assures us, that believers, after death, enter into life eternal, and that the punishment of the wicked will be everlasting [Matt. xxv. 46.; Dan. xii. 2.; 2 Thes. i. 7-10.].

I have now given you a summary of the great truths, which, as a minister of the gospel, I am commissioned and commanded to preach. And I can call God and your consciences to witness, that I have not shunned thus to declare to you the whole counsel of God [Acts xx. 27.]. I have explained to you the meaning, and I have urged the importance of these things over and over. I have pointed out to you, the wretched and dangerous condition of sinners, the necessity of conversion or the new birth, the nature of this change, and by what power it is wrought, and the fruits and effects which such a change will produce in a man's tempers, words and actions. I have also shewn you the way, in which you MAY and must be saved, if you are saved at all. I have told you again and again, that Christ is the Way, the truth, and the life, and that there is no coming to God with comfort, either in this world, or in that which is to come, but by him. He has told you so himself [John xiv. 6.; Acts iv. 12.]. And the apostle assures you, that there is no other name under heaven, given unto men, whereby they can be saved. Look unto him, and you shall be saved; if not, you must be damned. This is the plain truth, the express declaration of the Bible. Life and death are set before you [Deut. xxx. 15.].

Permit me then, as your minister, your friend, and a well-wisher to your souls, to press these serious and weighty considerations home upon your consciences once more. I hope and believe that I have affected nothing, but what can be proved by the highest authority, the word of the living God. They certainly deserve your closest and most careful attention, since it is plain beyond a doubt, that upon your knowledge or ignorance, your acceptance or rejection of this gospel, your everlasting happiness or misery must depend.

Brethren, I do not ask you, what religious persuasion or denomination you have espoused. I fear, that, if I may judge of your hearts by your actions, too many are destitute of any sense of religion at all. But I do not address you as Churchmen or Dissenters, Roman Catholics or Protestants, as Jews or Gentiles; I suppose, yea, I know, that there are persons of every denomination amongst you. But I speak to you as men and women, as intelligent creatures, possessed of understanding and reason. I speak to you as mortals, and yet immortals; as sinners, who have broken the laws of God, and are therefore obnoxious to his displeasure. And my sole aim and desire is, to be instrumental in turning you from darkness to light, from sin to holiness, from the power of Satan to the service and favour of God [Acts xxvi. 18.].

Seek then, I beseech you, above all things, an interest in the blessings of the gospel. Be assured it is a matter of much less moment, whether you are rich or poor, respected or despised in this world. The rich have their cares, fears, crosses, and vexations, no less than the poor; but admitting that they could pass through life with greater ease than others, we all know that they cannot escape death. The great point is, how we shall die? whether as believers or unbelievers, as saints or sinners. One soul, according to our Lord's declaration, is of more value than the whole world [Mark viii. 36.]. If you lose your soul, you lose all at once. You lose heaven and happiness for ever. Whatever, therefore, you do, or leave undone, for God's sake, and for your own sakes, neglect not for one day or hour longer, the vast concerns of another life. Delays are dangerous. The more we have to risk or lose, the greater folly it would be accounted, to defer securing our property and goods, which we know to be in danger. What folly, therefore, what madness must it be, to put off with careless indifference, the concernments of eternity; and to prefer the trifles of this transitory life to heaven, and the favour of God! Let the parable of the rich man, who pleased himself with the thought of having much good laid up for many years, be a warning to you![Luke xii. 16-28.] That very night his soul was required of him. Such persons may now deem themselves wise; but ere long they will be sensible they were fools.

It you consider what a valuable price was paid for our redemptions you must be convinced that the soul of man is very precious in the sight of God, and that sin is not so light and small an evil, as many of you have supposed. To disobey the commandments of the just and holy God, is, as far as in us lies, to renounce our allegiance to him, and our dependence upon him, and to set up for ourselves, and even to join with the devil in open rebellion against our Maker. It is, in plain terms, to fly in his face, and to bid defiance to his almighty arm. Sin is such a horrid evil, that unless it is forgiven, and blotted out, by the blood of Jesus, it will sink your souls lower than the center of the earth, even into the very depths of hell, never, never, never more to rise [Mark ix. 44-48].

So heinous was sin, in the sight of God, that rather than permit it to pass unpunished, he would punish it in the person of his own, his only, his well-beloved Son, who was made sin, that is, treated as a sinner deserved to be treated, for us. He was delivered up into the hands of wicked men, and crucified, that by his suffering and death, he might make atonement for our sins, and procure an honourable and happy reconciliation, between a righteous God, and offending sinners [2 Cor. v. 18-20]. I beseech you, therefore, to prize and to study this gospel, that you may obtain a growing experience of its benefits. Praise God for such a Saviour, and such a salvation as he has provided. Adore him, for that infinite wisdom, and boundless mercy which he has displayed in the redemption of fallen man and never rest, nor be satisfied, till you have good and scriptural reason to hope, that this Saviour is yours, with all the blessings he is exalted to bestow without money and without price.

Our food, my brethren, then only can nourish us, when it is eaten and digested. Medicines can only profit us, by being applied and taken. It is exactly thus with the gospel. We may hear, and talk of these things, but so long as they remain matters of speculation, and do not enter into our hearts, into the very vitals of our souls, (if I may so speak) we cannot be the better for them. Christ is the bread of life. His flesh is meat indeed, and his blood is drink indeed! But unless we ourselves do SPIRITUALLY eat the flesh and drink the blood of the Son of man (for our Lord speaks of food for the soul, not for the body) we have no life in us [John vi. 52-58.].

Moses, by the express command of God, erected a brazen serpent upon a pole, in the view of the camp of Israel [Numb. xxi. 9.]. Such of the people as were stung by the fiery serpents, were directed and commanded to look up to the brazen serpent. They who did so were healed. But if any resisted, they were sure to die. For no other means or physicians could relieve them. In like manner Christ Jesus our Saviour, once lifted up on the cross, is exhibited in the preaching of the gospel. Sinners, who are wounded and diseased by sin, are directed, exhorted, encouraged, and commanded to look up to him [John iii. 14, 15.]. And they who are persuaded so to do, are infallibly cured of all those spiritual maladies, under which they have long and sorely laboured. But all, who despise and reject this sovereign remedy of God's gracious appointment, either by a total indifference to religion, or by expecting salvation in any other way, will be left, and that most deservedly, to perish in their wilful obstinacy and unbelief [John iii, 36.].

PART II

In the former part of this address, I have already laid before you, in the plainest manner I was able, my views of the gospel of Christ. And as an experimental knowledge of this gospel is so very important, I have endeavoured to press that importance upon your consciences. Whether you have paid that attention to the subject, which it deserves and requires, yourselves best know. I can only say, that if I did not know it to be of great weight, I should not either speak or write of it with so much earnestness. But being persuaded and assured, by the express testimony of the holy scriptures, that these things are true; and truths, the knowledge of which is essential to your present and future happiness, I must be plain and faithful in declaring them. I ought to be very indifferent what men of depraved morals, and corrupt principles may say, or think of me, if I have the witness of a good conscience, and the approbation of the God whom I serve. My concern is for YOUR welfare and salvation; for I am certain, as I have told you before, and now tell you again, that unless the gospel is made the power of God to your souls, you must be miserable in time, and to eternity.

I propose now to give you some advices, to assist you in understanding the gospel for yourselves, which if you observe, I trust, you will attain to the possession of those principles, and walk by those rules, which will both afford you present peace, and secure your future happiness. For godliness has promises pertaining to the life that now is, and to that which is to come.

Let me then exhort you to attend seriously to what you are to believe; and to what you are to do. These two points include the sum and substance of the gospel, the whole of the christian life, and may be comprised in two words, FAITH and PRACTICE.

I. You must learn from the word of God, what you are to believe. True faith is the root and foundation of all real religion. Without this inward principle, nothing that we have done, or can do, will be acceptable to God [Heb. xi. 6.]. I have briefly informed you what you are to believe—That you are sinners, that Jesus Christ is an all-sufficient and willing Saviour—and that the word of God both warrants and commands you to look to him for salvation. This looking unto Jesus, is what we particularly mean by faith or believing. When we cordially and entirely rely upon him, upon the invitation of the promises of God, for pardon, peace, and eternal life, then we believe.

All who thus believe, through grace, are required and commanded to be careful of maintaining good works [Titus. iii. 8.]. As our moral, and what are often called, our virtuous actions, are to be tried by our religious principles; it is equally true, that our religious principles or at least the proof that they are indeed OUR principles, must be evidenced by our moral conduct. These two are so inseparably connected, that you may depend upon it, where one of them is wanting, what bears the name of the other, is no better than pretended. If what we profess to believe does not make us humble, honest, chaste, patient, and thankful, and regulate our tempers and behaviour, whatever good opinion we may form of our notions or state, we are but deceiving ourselves. The tree is known by its fruits [James. ii. 17,18.; Matt. vii. 20.]. In this way true believers are equally distinguished from profane sinners, and from specious hypocrites. The change in their hearts always produces a change in their whole deportment. Sin, which was once their delight, is now the object of their hatred. It was once necessary as their food, but now they avoid it as poison. They war, watch, and pray against it. And their delight is to study the revealed will of God.

By these tests you may judge of your true state before God. Surely you cannot suppose that your inward state is GOOD, while your outward conduct is BAD. Hence you may be assured that no unclean person, or profane swearer, no one who lives in direct opposition to the commands of God, can be, while he continues in this course, a true christian. Such a supposition would be no less absurd, than it would be to suppose, that a man is a good and peaceable subject, though he lives in open rebellion against the king. You may as well conceive of a holy devil, as of an unholy christian.

I hope you will not mistake me. I do not mean that true christians are without sin. But I affirm, that no true christian can live in an habitual course of sin. No, sin is their grief, their burden [1 John. iii. 8,9.; Rom. vii. 23,24.]; and when through temptation, or unwatchfulness, they are drawn aside, like the dove sent out of the ark, they can find no rest, till by hearty repentance, and true faith, they obtain a new sense of forgiveness.

I now proceed to offer you some directions, with which if you comply, I trust, that by the blessing of God, you will enjoy peace in your souls, and be enabled to regulate your conduct and conversation, as becometh the gospel of Christ.

Read and study the scriptures. This was our Lord's direction to the Jews. Search the scriptures, for in them ye think ye have eternal life, and they testify of me [John v. 37; Acts xvii. 11.]. The Bereans were commended for their attention and diligence in this respect. They received the word with all readiness of mind, not with a blind and implicit faith in what they heard, even from an apostle, but they searched the scriptures daily, to know whether what he taught them was agreeable to the word of God.

The Bible is our only sure and infallible guide. It was given by inspiration of God. All other books, however good and useful, are but of human composition, and are therefore not perfect. [2 Tim. 8-16.; Isa. viii. 20.]

This sacred book, as I have already observed to you, contains all that is needful to make us wise unto salvation. It informs us of our original, how pure and innocent; and our present condition, how guilty, polluted and miserable! and the happiness or misery which awaits us in a future state. From this book we may learn, the malignity of sin, the holiness, spirituality, extent, and sanction of the law of God; and consequently, the just and certain condemnation due to our disobedience. It shews us, likewise, the way of our recovery. How perfectly the mediation of Christ is suited to vindicate the honour of the law, and to display the justice of God, in harmony with his mercy, and thereby to give peace to the consciences of convinced sinners.

I intreat you, therefore, to read the word of God carefully. Many of you have had Bibles or New Testaments given to you, and others might have them, if they had but an inclination to read.

Some of you will perhaps object, and say, as you have already said to me, We cannot read. Others, We have no time given us. If you cannot read yourselves, you might prevail on some of your comrades to read to you*. As to your having no time, I much question it. Rather you have no inclination. Too many of you can find time to jest, to talk obscenely or profanely, to read and sing idle songs; why might not some, or rather the whole of this time be employed in reading, or hearing the Bible? You might find time, if you could find a will. But remember, that such excuses as you now make, will stand you in no stead when you appear before God in judgment. There are few, if any of you, but might have opportunity of attending to these things, if you were but willing.

[*Footnote: Two or three hours thus spent on the Lord's day, in instructing each other to read, would be a very commendable employment. I have often expressed my longing desire that such a plan was set on foot among you. And if there could be a convenient building created for this purpose, I should think myself happy, not only to furnish you with books, as far as I am able, but also personally to attend and assist you, as much as my immediate calls of duty would permit.]

II. Observe and reverence the sabbath, or Lord's day. Remember the sabbath-day, to keep it holy [Exod. xx. 8.], is a solemn and positive command of God. To live in the neglect of this commandment, is absolutely to despise God, and to defy him, as it were to his face. Consider, my friends, you have orders frequently given you here, by your superiors, which you know you must obey, or you know the consequences of disobedience—judge then for yourselves, what have those persons to expect, who, in defiance of the authority of the great

God, presume to neglect and profane the day which he has so expressly enjoined to be kept holy?

It gives me a deep and continual concern to observe how the Lord's-day is spent by many of you. What would a stranger think, who regards the sabbath, if he visited every part of this colony on the Lord's day? Ah! my brethren, I have seen and heard enough (alas! much more than enough) to form my own judgment on this subject. If my duty did not require my attendance on the public worship, and were I to visit your different places and huts, I fear I should find some of you spending the hours appointed for divine service in cultivating your gardens and grounds, others indulging themselves in mere sloth and idleness, others engaged in the most profane and unclean conversation, and others committing abominations, which it would defile my pen to describe. Now what must be the end of these courses? God says, Remember the sabbath day to keep it holy. But the language, both of your hearts and actions, is, "We will not keep it holy. It is a day given us for ourselves; and we wish, and we are resolved to spend it as we please. We do not chuse to be confined, or compelled to hear so much preaching and praying." Is not this the language of your hearts? Your conduct too plainly proves it: but, my brethren, let me reason and expostulate a little with you upon this head.

Consider, what have been the consequences to many who have thus broken God's commands. I have known, and you likewise have known, those who have been brought to an untimely and disgraceful end, and who have dated their ruin from this one evil, the profanation of the Lord's day. Instead of spending it in the manner which he has enjoined, they kept bad and profligate company. By this practice, all serious impressions (if they formerly had any) have been driven from their minds. Their hearts have become more and more hardened and insensible; till at length, lost to all prudent reflection, they have regarded neither the tender solicitations and tears of parents, relations, and friends, the faithful warnings of ministers, nor the checks and rebukes of their own consciences. And what has been the event? I need not tell you, that having given way to their own wicked wills, the advice and example of their ungodly companions, and the temptations of the devil (for, be assured, that he is always at the bottom of these mischiefs) they have, at length, committed some act of depredation and villainy, which has brought them to an untimely grave.

Such, brethren, have been the free and ingenuous confessions of many of those unhappy people who have suffered death. And if you were to speak the sentiments of your hearts, I doubt not, but many of you, who by the mercy of God are yet living, would make the like acknowledgment; that breaking the sabbath was the first step towards bringing you into that pitiable situation, in which you either have been, or still are suffering. And will you still persevere in the road of misery? Will you still prefer the chains of your own depraved inclinations, to the service of God, which is perfect freedom? According to the Jewish law, a man was stoned to death, for gathering sticks on the sabbath day [Numb. xv. 32-36.], whereas you are doing a number of things on the Lord's day, which might as well be done before, or left undone till afterwards. But such is the long-suffering of the Lord, that though others have been cut off, you are spared to this hour. May his goodness lead you to repentance! Or otherwise, light as these things may appear to you now, and though you may plead a necessity for what you do, I tell you again, as I have often told you before, that a day is coming when God will call you to a strict account.

Besides, If you would reasonably hope for the blessing of God to succeed your labours, it is certainly your interest, as well as your duty to obey his commands. And this in particular, Keep the sabbath day holy. If, in direct opposition to this plain, precept, you will work and labour, as on other days, what ground can you have to expect that God will bless and prosper your undertakings? You have much greater cause to fear that his curse will follow you in your affairs, and blast and disappoint all your wishes and prospects.

Let then the misconduct and fatal ends of others, and the calamities and troubles that you have brought upon yourselves—Let the gracious promises of God, on the one hand, and his awful threatenings on the other, induce you, in future, to remember the sabbath day, to keep it holy!

And let me offer you a few plain directions, as to the observance and improvement of the sabbath:

Begin the day with prayer; and for this purpose seek some place of retirement, if you find it impracticable to meditate or pray, from the interruptions you are exposed to in your dwellings*, from those who ridicule and scoff at every appearance of religion. Retire from them, and pray to him who seeth in secret; and praise him for the many mercies you have received. Consider with yourself, how little you have improved them. Humble yourselves before God, under a sense of your sins and imperfections, and pray for pardon and repentance. Intreat him, to enable you to watch over your hearts, words, and actions, throughout the day, and that you may not be hindered or hurt by the snares and temptations around you. Intreat God to assist your minister, and to accompany what you may hear from him, with a blessing to your soul, and to all who shall be present with you.

[*Footnote: Many complaints have been made to me on this head.]

If you have families, you should call them together, and pray with them, and for them. There are many promises made to worshiping families, and to those who, like Abraham, endeavour to teach their children and household to know and serve the Lord. [Gen. xviii. 19.; Prov. iii. 33.] And the neglect of this is one reason, why many families live uncomfortably. They live without prayer, and therefore without peace.

Having thus endeavoured to impress your minds with serious thoughts, in secret or at home; attend constantly upon the public worship, and there pay a close attention to every part of the service. Remember that the eye of God is particularly upon you there. He has promised to be with two or three that meet together to call upon his name [Matt. xviii. 20.; John iv. 24]. He is to be worshipped in spirit and in truth; and whether they assemble in a church, or in the open air, he can give them cause to say with Jacob, This place is surely the house of God, and the gate of Heaven [Gen. xxviii. 17.]. Attend the public worship again in the afternoon, with your hearts lifted up to God, that you may not hear in vain; and accustom yourself in the evening to recollect what you have heard, concerning the miseries which sin has brought into the world, the love of God in sending his own Son to redeem sinners from those miseries; the sufferings, life, death, and resurrection of the Saviour; and that eternal rest, which remaineth for the people of God—FOR YOU, and FOR ME, if we are believers in Christ.

If, by the blessing of God, I can happily persuade you thus to observe and improve the Lord's day, I am sure it will promote both your pleasure and your profit. Can it be a question with you, whether the God who made heaven and earth, or Satan, the god of this world, is the best master? Indeed I too well know the indisposition and averseness of the carnal mind to God and his ways. Hence the thought of many is, What a weariness is it? And, When will the sabbath be ended? Hence that open contempt and scorn, which is cast upon the sabbath, and upon public worship by many, both high and low, rich and poor, bond and free, old and young, men and women. To them the worship of God is tedious and disagreeable. They neither find pleasure in it, nor expect benefit from it. And therefore their attendance is not from choice, but from constraint.

But the thoughts and the conduct of true Christians are very different. No day is so welcome to them as the Lord's day; not merely considered as a day of rest from labour; but because, having their heads and hearts freed from the cares and incumbrances of the world, it affords them opportunities of waiting upon God. And, brethren, you must allow that these persons are best qualified to judge of the question I have proposed, Whether is best, to walk in the ways of God, or in the ways of sin? For they have experienced both sides of the question. They have tried the pleasures of the world, and they have also tried the pleasures of religion. And they will readily assure you, that in their deliberate judgment, one day thus spent in devotion, and the exercises of religion, is preferable to a thousand days wasted in the vain and unsatisfying pleasures, which they sought in their former wicked practices [Ps. lxxxiv. 10.].

I have written thus largely upon the due observance of the Lord's day, because of that shameful, open, and general neglect, that daring profanation of the Sabbath, which abounds amongst us. It is well known, and it is matter of great grief and concern to me, that numbers of you pay not the least regard to this day. Numbers of you will not come to public worship at all, others but seldom, and then with much reluctance. And when spoken to, different persons frame different excuses, all which, when examined, amount to little more than a want of inclination.

I have here a more special reference to those of you, who are called Settlers and Free People. You think, perhaps, and some of you say, That having served out your appointed term, you are now your own masters, and have therefore a right to employ your time as you please. But, indeed, it is not so. I must tell you, brethren, that my commission from God, and my appointment from government, extend equally and alike to all the inhabitants, without distinction. It is my duty to preach to all, to pray for all, and to admonish every one. And it is no less the duty of all, to come to public worship, to hear the gospel, and to pray for me. These mutual ties and obligations between you and me, are not lessened by any change in your circumstances. And remember, that the slight you put upon the public worship, is not properly a slight of me (if that was all, it would be a matter of utter indifference) but upon the Lord himself; for I trust it is his message, and not my own, that I deliver to you [Luke x. 16.]. I wish, therefore, what I have said upon this subject, to be understood as addressed TO ALL, whether of higher or lower rank, who are guilty of breaking the sabbath. Whatever our station or calling may be, our obligations to keep holy the sabbath-day, are precisely the same. If any are more inexcusable than the rest, it must be those, who, from their station and office, are peculiarly bound to set a good example to others. I hope this friendly hint will be received in good part. I mean not to offend. But I must admonish you, that whatever be your situation in life, you will gain nothing in the end, by doing what God forbids, nor will you be a loser by yielding strict obedience to his commands.

III. Be constant and diligent in prayer to God. Intreat him to give his blessing to what you read and hear, and to all your concerns. As we are weak and needy creatures, always dependent upon God, and always receiving mercies and favours from him, we ought to be frequent and earnest in prayer. Daniel was accustomed to pray three times in the day [Dan. vi. 10.; Ephes. ii. 12.]. I hope you will be punctual in prayer, morning and evening, at least. So long as any of you live without prayer, you live without Christ, without hope, and without God in the world. They, who do not pray to God while upon earth, will not be admitted to praise him in heaven. When the rich careless man who had fared sumptuously every day, for a time, lifted up his eyes in torments, he only desired and prayed for a drop of water to cool his tongue, but it was not granted to him. Oh! if you value your souls, pray earnestly to God. Consider your obligations to do so. He is your Creator, Preserver, Benefactor. In him you live and move, and have your being. And therefore not to acknowledge, by prayer, your dependence upon him, would manifest the greatest ingratitude and insensibility. Consider, likewise, the encouragement you have to pray. Though you are by nature sinners, and by practice enemies and rebels, he gives you free and sure promises, that whoever is disposed to return to him, and seek him by earnest prayer, shall not seek him in vain. Oh! my brethren, that there was less cursing and swearing, and more prayer among you!

After these positive directions what you ought TO DO, I proceed to some necessary cautions, against what you ought to avoid.

I. Profane swearing is one thing against which I am especially bound to warn you, because it is an evil which so much abounds amongst you.

God has said, Thou shalt not take the name of the Lord thy God in vain, for the Lord will not hold him guiltless, that taketh his name in vain. Our Saviour likewise has said, Swear not at all [Exod. xx. 7.; Matt. v. 34.]. But how can you reconcile these prohibitions to your conduct; or your consciences? When instead of not swearing at all, many of you seldom open your lips, but the first and last words which you utter, are blasphemous oaths, and horrid imprecations? Is this acting like rational or accountable creatures? Who gave you the powers of reason and speech? Was it not God? And can you think that he gave them to you, that you may blaspheme his holy name, and to use the most profane, obscene, and desperately wicked language your hearts can invent; a language only fit for incarnate devils, and shocking to the ears of the ignorant heathens? This is a dreadful evil which you may be assured, will not pass unpunished. This sin has often brought heavy judgments upon individuals, families, and kingdoms. Because of swearing the land mourneth [Jer. xxiii. 10]. Shall not I visit for these things, saith the Lord?

As a proof of the enormity of this sin, you read, that Moses, by the command of God, ordered a man to be stoned to death, for cursing and blaspheming [Lev. xxiv. 10-16.]; and it would be well, both on their own account, and for the good of others, if magistrates would strictly discharge their duty, by enforcing the laws of our land, which are engaged against this horrid practice. And in few places, perhaps in no place, such strictness would be more needful, or more salutary, than in this colony.

Our Lord assures us, that for every idle word that men shall speak they shall give an account in the day of judgment! [Matt. xii. 36] How dreadful then will be the case of those persons, who during their whole life have employed their tongues in cursing, swearing, lying, and all manner of vile and unclean conversation. Oh! think of this in time, and tremble and repent, and learn to use your tongues to better purpose in future! Read carefully the third chapter of James, and pray to God for his grace, and use your best endeavours to bridle your tongues which, if you do not subdue and conquer, will surely destroy and ruin you.

II. Consider, also, what must be the consequence of that unclean and adulterous course of life, which many of you follow. Common as this wickedness is in our colony (I believe no where more so) do not suppose, that the frequency will take away, or in the least abate the criminality of it. Neither suppose that this sin is less odious in the sight of God if committed in Port Jackson, than in England. You may frame excuses or plead necessity, for what you do, or permit to be done; but the word of God by which you must be at last judged, admits, of no plea, or excuse. The command is positive and absolute. The declaration of God, Thou shalt not commit adultery [Exod. xx. 14], is equally binding upon persons of all ranks to whom it is known, at all times, and in all places. Think not, that the holy and just God will dispense with his law, or relax the sentence he has denounced against the breach of it, that you may with impunity indulge your corrupt desires. No; it is written, whoremongers and adulterers God will judge. The apostle declares that no fornicator, adulterer, or unclean person, can enter into the kingdom of God; he repeats this warning nearly in the same words, a second and a third time. The heavens and the earth shall pass away; but not one jot or tittle of his word can fail. All shall be fulfilled [Heb. xiii. 4.; Gal. v. 17-21.; Eph. v. 3-5.]. And therefore, however this sin may be connived at by some, and committed by others, God will severely punish offenders, unless they repent of their wickedness and forsake it.

But I need not enlarge upon this subject, I have told you my thoughts of it again and again with faithfulness. It seems the plainness of my language has hurt the delicate feelings of some, and the faithfulness I have used has excited the censure and ill-will of others. But why am I blamed, if I have only affirmed and proved from the scriptures, that no fornicator, adulterer, or unclean person can go to heaven WHEN HE DIES, unless he repents of his evil practices, and turns from them, WHILE HE LIVES?

But whether you will hear, or whether you will forbear, I must repeat the unwelcome truth. My conscience, my duty, and my compassion, all urge me to deal faithfully with you. I mean and desire to be understood, and therefore I must speak plainly. It is my intention and desire to awaken and alarm your consciences: but alas! after all I can say or do, I am too little understood or regarded. But I must deliver my own soul, whether you will regard me or not. The day is coming when the Lord himself will judge between you and me. Oh, repent, repent, before it be too late.

III. The conduct of too many of you induces me to exhort and caution you farther against theft, and all kinds of dishonesty and villainy.

I have often told you, both publicly and privately, that honesty is the best policy. None have more reason to be convinced of this, than you who come hither as convicts. You have known by bitter experience, the unhappy consequences of dishonesty. Have not many of you, for the sake, perhaps, of a few shillings, unjustly obtained, plunged yourselves into misery for the remainder of your lives? Several have made this acknowledgment to me, in their dying moments. Learn therefore, strive, and pray to be honest. Honesty has its present advantages. An honest man, however poor, can face this world with confidence. But a dishonest behaviour, with its constant attendant a guilty conscience, will always fill the mind with fear and dismay. [Job. xxiv. 16,17.]

I do not mean, my friends, to reflect harshly upon you for what is past, and cannot be recalled. I pity your past misconduct; I sympathize with you under your present sufferings. And therefore I admonish and caution you to abstain from this course for the time to come. Let then the troubles and afflictions you have brought upon yourselves be a warning, to regulate your future behaviour. Learn to be thankful for what God in his providence gives you, whether it be more or less. Attend to what our Lord says, Whatsoever ye would that men should do unto you, do ye even so unto them. And to his apostle's direction, Let him that hath stolen, steal no more, but rather let him labour, working with his hands the thing which is good, that he may have to give to him that needeth [Matt. vii. 12.; Eph. iv. 24.]. Follow this advice, and you will soon experience the benefit.

IV. Beware of idleness. This is the forerunner of many evils. Poverty, disease, disgrace, misery, and too often an untimely death, are the consequences of sloth and indolence. Yield not to idleness; if you indulge it, you will find it grow upon you. Therefore, be diligent and industrious in your lawful callings. It is written in the Bible, and confirmed by experience and observation, The idle soul shall suffer hunger, but the soul of the diligent shall be made fat. [Prov. xix. 15. & xiii. 14.]

V. Be careful also to pay due respect, submission, and obedience to your superiors. It is the good pleasure of God that some should be placed in more exalted, and others in a more humble station. And it is a proof of his wisdom and goodness. The present state of the world, and the general good of mankind, render such distinctions necessary. But whether we are high or low, whether called to command, or required to obey, our duties and obligations are mutual. It is in society as in the human body. There are many members, and every member has its proper place, and its proper office. Let every soul be subject to the higher powers [Rom. xiii. 1.].

I have thus given you my best advice respecting what you ought to do, or to avoid. Permit me to invite your serious attention to what I have written. Consider it carefully FOR YOUR OWN SAKES. It concerns your PRESENT comfort. For though no works of ours, or what are called, moral virtues, can possibly procure us the favour of God, (for our best services are imperfect and defiled, and need forgiveness) yet that knowledge and experience of the gospel, which I have explained to you in the first part of this Address, (and of which I earnestly pray you may be made partakers) must be accompanied by a correspondent conduct, such as I have set before you in the second part. And this knowledge and this conduct will always be attended, though not always in the same degree, with an inward settled peace, whereby the mind is reconciled to support crosses and afflictions, however great, or of long continuance, with a degree of fortitude and resignation. Persons under this influence will say, when they meet with troubles, I will bear the indignation of the Lord, because I have sinned against him [Micah. vii. 9.]. Should it please God, to answer the earnest desire of my soul, by giving you an experience of the gospel peace, you will thank and praise him, even for bringing you hither; and you will see and confess, that your heaviest afflictions have, in the event, proved to be your greatest mercies.

Your FUTURE comfort and welfare in this world, depends upon this knowledge. For though no one knows what may befal him in this life, yet the real christian has the comfort of knowing, that however it may go with the wicked, or whatever may happen to himself of a temporal nature, or whatever may become of his body, he is sure (because God has promised) that it shall be well with his soul at death. Ah! my brethren, then, more especially then, believers will find the advantage of having made the word of God the foundation of their hope, and the rule of their life!

Several of you, some to my knowledge, have left affectionate, tender, and serious friends, husbands, wives, parents, brothers, sisters, or children, in your native country, to lament your misconduct, the sufferings you have brought upon yourselves, and the disgrace in which you have involved your families. Let me intreat you, FOR THE SAKE OF THESE, to consider your ways. Great comfort it will afford to those who are now almost overwhelmed with grief on your account, to hear of your reformation and conversion. These would be glad tidings, indeed, from a far country. The hopes they might then form of seeing you again, would be truly pleasing; it would be little less than receiving you again from the dead. Or if they never see you in this world, the prospect of meeting with you in heaven, would add comfort to their dying hours. Oh! let not their prayers and their tears be lost upon you!

Attend to these things, FOR THE SAKE OF OTHERS, who may follow you hither, in the like unhappy circumstances. When they see your reformation, and that in consequence of it, you are more comfortable here than you were at home, they may be induced and encouraged to follow your examples. Thus you will be instrumental in saving souls from death.

I would farther plead with you, for the sake of the poor unenlightened savages, who daily visit us, or who reside amongst us. If these ignorant natives, as they become more and more acquainted with our language and manners, hear you, many of you, curse, swear, lie, abound in every kind of obscene and profane conversation; and if they observe, that it is common with you to steal, to break the sabbath, to be guilty of uncleanness, drunkenness, and other abominations; how must their minds become prejudiced and their hearts hardened against that pure and holy religion which we profess? Oh beware of laying stumbling-blocks in the way of these blind people [Lev. xix. 14.], lest the blood of their souls be one day required at your hands.

And yet I fear, yea, I well know, that they have already heard and seen too much of such language, and such practices amongst us.

Already some of them have been taught to speak such language as they continually hear, and though they do not yet understand the meaning of the words they use, they can utter oaths and blasphemies almost as readily as their CHRISTIAN instructors. By-standers divert themselves with their attempts in this way, and think it is fine sport. But, my friends, the scripture declares they are fools who make a mock at sin.[Prov. xiv. 9.] But these things cause much sorrow to those who have any reverence for God, or pity for their fellow creatures. I readily profess my own deep concern for these proceedings, and my utter abhorrence of them. And I most earnestly intreat you, if you cannot instruct them in what is better, to have no communication at all with them. For if you make them partakers of your sins, you must answer for it at the great day of judgment; if they then rise up against you, for misleading them, it will be much more tolerable for them than for you.

But consider, on the other hand, what may be the happy effects, were the natives to see, hear, and observe in you, and in all the Europeans here; in ministers and people, high and low, a conduct answerable to the doctrine and precepts of the gospel. This might, by the blessing of God, be one of the most effectual means, to bring them to reflection, and to engage them to seek an interest in the blessings of the gospel for themselves.

Shall I beg and intreat you, FOR MY SAKE, to attend to the things pertaining to your true peace. My dear people, I will again declare (I can appeal to the great God, who searcheth the hearts, that I speak the truth) to see you converted from your evil ways, and seeking the salvation of God, Yes, to see you pay a due regard to these most important concerns, and to have reason to hope and believe, that you were brought to a saving acquaintance with the truths which you hear of, or might hear, as often as the Lord's day returns, would indeed greatly rejoice my soul. But to see so many of you turn a careless and deaf ear, this, my dear friends, is a cause of great, constant and increasing grief to my soul. It wounds me to think, that any (alas! what numbers) should thus refuse and reject their own mercies; and risk the ruin of their immortal souls, for the prospect of a small gain, or a short sinful gratification.

My brethren, what shall I, what can I say more. I neither know what to add, nor how to leave off: once more, I beseech you, for God's sake, for the sake of Jesus the Saviour, who shed his precious blood to redeem sinners, and for the sake of your own souls: by the holy incarnation of the Redeemer, by his agonies, temptations, death and resurrection, by all the terrors of his frown, and by all the blessings of his love, by the joys of heaven, by the torments of hell, and by the solemnities of the approaching day of judgment; by all these considerations, I most earnestly, affectionately, and faithfully admonish and intreat you, carefully to weigh what I have now set before you. And oh! that the holy angels may carry to heaven the joyful news [Luke xv. 10.] of some sinners being awakened and born to God, by reading or hearing this little book. O gracious God, do thou, by the power of thy Holy Spirit, make it thus effectual to the salvation and happiness of this people!

And now to this gracious Lord, and to his care and blessing, I commend you. May he enable you to examine your hearts, principles, and practice, by the standard of his holy word. If you are still ignorant and careless, it is a proof that you are, as yet, in the state of nature, which is a state of darkness, guilt, condemnation, and death. Will you not pray to be delivered from it? You must, at least, allow, that perhaps what you have read, MAY BE the truth. And even, of a possibility of these things being true, they deserve your earnest attention. For should they be found so at last, what will become of you, if you live and die impenitent? Therefore, read this plain, affectionate Address seriously. Read it a second, a third, and a fourth time, till your hearts are affected by it. Remember, this is the advice of a friend, of one who sincerely seeks, wishes, and longs for your happiness. It is the advice of your minister, expressly appointed to watch over your souls, and who must shortly give an account of his mission to the Great judge of all. Whether I shall die amongst you, or be separated from you while living, we shall, at last, meet before him. Then I must answer for my preaching, and you for your hearing. Oh that this awful day of judgment may be often, yea, always, present to your thoughts, and to mine! that we may live in constant expectation of its approach! So that when the last loud trumpet shall sound, we may stand with acceptance and boldness in his presence, and be admitted as believers in the great Saviour, into his heavenly kingdom, with a 'Well done, good and faithful servant, enter thou into the joy of thy Lord.'[Matt. xxv. 23.]

This will be my daily prayer to God for you. I shall pray for your eternal salvation, for your present welfare, for the preservation, peace, and prosperity of this colony: and especially for the more abundant and manifest success of the Redeemer's cause and kingdom, and for the effusion and out-pouring of his Holy Spirit, not only here, but in every part of the habitable globe. Longing, hoping, and waiting for the dawn of that happy day, when the heathen shall be given to the Lord Jesus for his inheritance, and the uttermost parts of the earth for his possession: and when all the ends of the earth shall see, believe, and rejoice in the salvation of God. [Ps. ii. 8. & xcviii. 3.]

I am your affectionate Friend and
Servant in the Gospel of Christ,

RICHARD JOHNSON.

FINIS.